BLESSED NAMES

WHY WAS HE NAMED AL-ASKARI (A)?

WRITTEN BY:

KISA KIDS PUBLICATIONS

Please recite a Fātiḥah for the marḥūmīn
of the Rangwala family, the sponsors of this book.

All proceeds from the sale of this book
will be used to produce more educational resources.

Dedication

This book is dedicated to the beloved Imām of our time (AJ). May Allāh (swt) hasten his reappearance and help us become his true companions.

Acknowledgements

Prophet Muḥammad (s): The pen of a writer is mightier than the blood of a martyr.

True reward lies with Allāh, but we would like to sincerely thank Shaykh Salim Yusufali and Sisters Sabika Mithar Liliana Villalvazo, Zahra Sabur, Kisae Nazar, Sarah Assaf, Nadia Dossani, Fatima Hussain, Naseem Rangwala, ar Zehra Abbas. We would especially like to thank Nainava Publications for their contributions. May Allāh bless them this world and the next.

Preface

Prophet Muḥammad (s): Nurture and raise your children in the best way. Raise them with the love of the Prophe and the Ahl al-Bayt (a).

Literature is an influential form of media that often shapes the thoughts and views of an entire generation. Therefor in order to establish an Islamic foundation for the future generations, there is a dire need for compelling Islam literature. Over the past several years, this need has become increasingly prevalent throughout Islamic centers ar schools everywhere. Due to the growing dissonance between parents, children, society, and the teachings of Islā and the Ahl al-Bayt (a), this need has become even more pressing. Al-Kisa Foundation, along with its subsidiar Kisa Kids Publications, was conceived in an effort to help bridge this gap with the guidance of 'ulamah and the help educators. We would like to make this a communal effort and platform. Therefore, we sincerely welcome constructi feedback and help in any capacity.

The goal of the *Blessed Names* series is to help children form a lasting bond with the 14 Mā'ṣūmīn by learni about and connecting with their names. We hope that you and your children enjoy these books and use them as means to achieve this goal, inshā'Allāh. We pray to Allāh to give us the strength and tawfīq to perform our duties ar responsibilities.

With Duʾās,
Nabi R. Mir (Abidi)

Kisa Kids Publications
4415 Fortran Court
San Jose, CA 95134
(260) KISA-KID [547-2543]

An Introduction to the Blessed Names

Our names are a very special part of us. Many times, they shape our personalities and even explain who we are or the person we would like to become. In this series, you will explore the names and titles of our beloved 14 Ma'soomeen. Did you know that their names and titles were not just ordinary names? They were special because they were given to them by Allah!

Allah has given seven special heavenly names to our Ma'soomeen: Muhammad, Ali, Fatimah, Hasan, Husain, Ja'far, and Musa. Behind each of these names is a heavenly power!

In addition to their names, each of the Ma'soomeen also had special titles by which they became famous. Their titles were often given to them because of the circumstances of their time, but these titles and characteristics were common amongst all the Ma'soomeen. For example, Imam al-Baqir (a) was known for spreading knowledge because he was able to create many new universities and branches of knowledge during his time. However, if the other Ma'soomeen had the same opportunity, they, too, would have spread knowledge and created universities in their teaching circles. In these stories, you will discover some of the reasons why the Ma'soomeen received their specific names or titles.

Many of us share our names with these beloved Ma'soomeen or know people who do. Let's learn about these blessed names and titles so we can strive to be like our blessed Ma'soomeen!

I think al-Askari means...

_____

It was a hot day in the desert of Medina. The commander watched the caravan and waited until the last few people had mounted onto their camels. He then rode his horse around the caravan to make sure all the luggage was packed and safely fastened to the camels. People from all the surrounding villages gathered around to say their last tearful goodbyes.

After a very long and tiring journey, the Imam (a) and his family finally reached Samarra safely. Imam al-Hadi (a) got down from his camel and walked towards his new home with his young son, Imam Hasan al-Askari (a).

The home that was chosen for the Imam (a) and his family was located on an army base. The area was called Askar, which means "army," and was surrounded by many homes of soldiers and commanders.

Imam Hasan al-Askari (a) grew up in the area of Askar. Life at the army base was difficult, especially for children. Often times, the loud noises of the horses and soldiers would startle them and keep them awake all night.

His house was like a prison. From behind the bars attached to his windows, all he would see were large soldiers with scary weapons. The children couldn't even play outside because it was so dangerous!

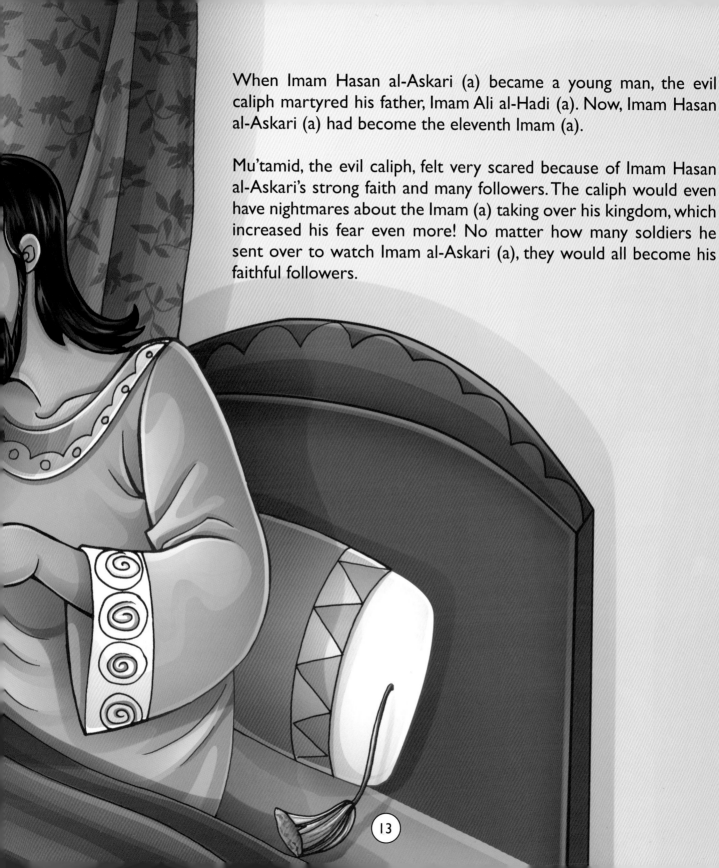

When Imam Hasan al-Askari (a) became a young man, the evil caliph martyred his father, Imam Ali al-Hadi (a). Now, Imam Hasan al-Askari (a) had become the eleventh Imam (a).

Mu'tamid, the evil caliph, felt very scared because of Imam Hasan al-Askari's strong faith and many followers. The caliph would even have nightmares about the Imam (a) taking over his kingdom, which increased his fear even more! No matter how many soldiers he sent over to watch Imam al-Askari (a), they would all become his faithful followers.

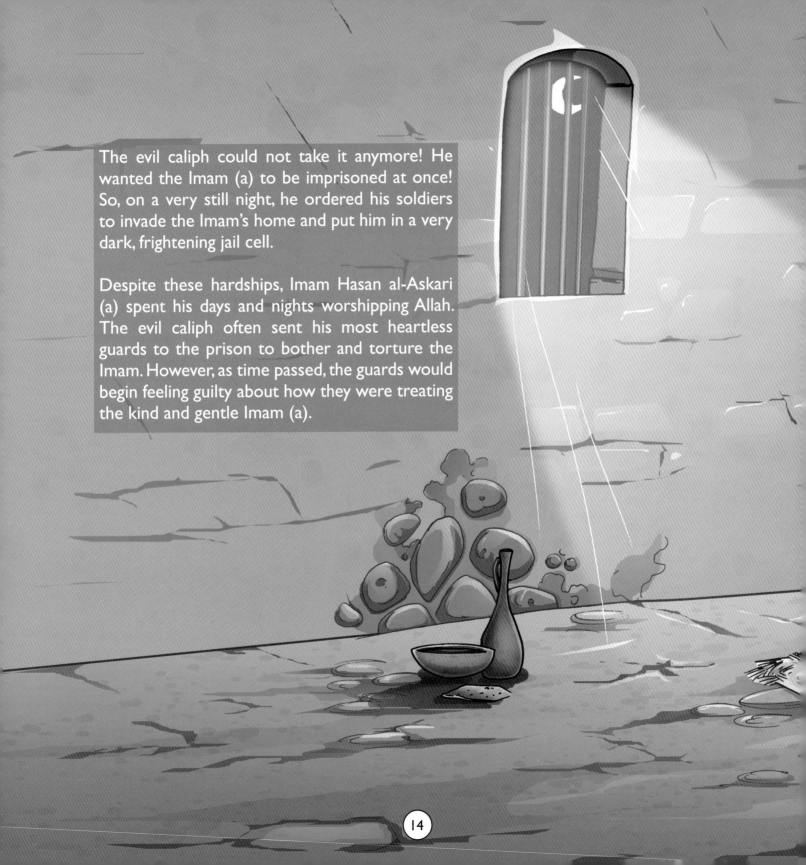

The evil caliph could not take it anymore! He wanted the Imam (a) to be imprisoned at once! So, on a very still night, he ordered his soldiers to invade the Imam's home and put him in a very dark, frightening jail cell.

Despite these hardships, Imam Hasan al-Askari (a) spent his days and nights worshipping Allah. The evil caliph often sent his most heartless guards to the prison to bother and torture the Imam. However, as time passed, the guards would begin feeling guilty about how they were treating the kind and gentle Imam (a).

One day, the caliph called two guards to his palace. He asked them how the Imam (a) was doing in prison. The two guards were very ashamed of what they were doing to the Imam (a) and said, "What can we say about a man who fasts during the day and prays all night? He spends his entire day and night worshipping Allah. When we hear him talking to Allah, tears come to our eyes, and we are unable to harm him." Angered, the caliph ordered new soldiers to go torture and bother the Imam (a).

However, anyone who would go to the prison and try to bother the Imam (a) would also fall in love with him and his akhlaq and not be able to hurt him.

The caliph could not take it anymore, so he put the Imam (a) under house arrest in Askar.

Imam Hasan al-Askari (a) spent most of his years in the area of Askar, which is why he is called "al-Askari, the soldier." Even though he was surrounded by many other soldiers, he was the one true soldier, since he only obeyed Allah.

Did you know that the Prophet (s) and Imams (a) had told their companions about this title years before Imam Hasan al-Askari (a) was even born or moved to Askar? This is because the title was given to him by Allah!

Even though Imam al-Askari (a) spent most of his life in prison or under house arrest, his followers and companions continued to grow over the years.

Finally, the caliph had had enough! He realized that too many people loved the Imam (a), so he decided to kill him! The caliph ordered someone to poison our beloved Imam al-Askari (a), making him a *shaheed*, or martyr, at the young age of 28. The Imamate was then transferred to his five-year-old son, Imam al-Mahdi (AJ), the twelfth and final Imam.

May Allah send His peace and blessings upon our beloved Imam Hasan al-Askari (a), who was a true soldier of Allah.

Ilal ash-Sharāiʿ, Vol. 1, P. 241
Kashf ul-Ghummah fi Maʿrifah al-Aʾimmah, Vol. 3, P. 290